No More Rent

The First-Time Buyer's Key To Unlocking Home Ownership

Andy Haynes

master plan focus publishing

Andy Haynes

LESS EXCUSES,
MORE RESULTS

© Copyright Andy Haynes 2023 - **All rights reserved.**

The content contained within this book may not be reproduced, duplicated, or transmitted without direct written permission from the author or the publisher.

Under no circumstances will any blame or legal responsibility be held against the publisher, or author, for any damages, reparation, or monetary loss due to the information contained within this book. Either directly or indirectly. You are responsible for your own choices, actions, and results.

Legal Notice:

This book is copyright protected. This book is only for personal use. You cannot amend, distribute, sell, use, quote or paraphrase any part, or the content within this book, without the consent of the author or publisher.

Disclaimer Notice:

Please note the information contained within this document is for educational and entertainment purposes only. All effort has been executed to present accurate, up to date, and reliable, complete information. No warranties of any kind are declared or implied. Readers acknowledge that the author is not engaging in the rendering of legal, financial, medical or professional advice. The content within this book has been derived from various sources. Please consult a suitably qualified professional before attempting any techniques outlined in this book.

By reading this document, the reader agrees that under no circumstances is the author responsible for any losses, direct or indirect, which are incurred as a result of the use of the information contained within this document, including, but not limited to, errors, omissions, or inaccuracies.

ISBN:

eBook: **9781915409164**

Paperback: **9781915409157**

Hardback: **9781915409096**

IMAGES:

Page xix: **ANDY HAYNES**
image by Emma Major

Page 1: **"POSSIBLE" CHALKBOARD**
image by Towfiqu Barbhuiya on Unsplash Jxi526YIQgA

Page 2: **HOUSE PRICES GRAPH**
image used with permission of Nationwide Building Society

Page 31: **WIZARDRY BOOK**
image licensed from iStock 516134724

Page 65: **NURTURE ROOM LAYOUT**
image by Spacejoy on Unsplash IH7wPsjwomc

Disclaimer

PLEASE TAKE THE TIME TO READ THIS SECTION AS IT CONTAINS IMPORTANT GUIDANCE:

The information you are about to see and read in this book is all believed to be correct at the time of publication. Of course, legislation changes laws over time, and this may mean some, or all, of these ideas may no longer be possible. However, it could also be the case that these principles become simpler to use.

Readers acknowledge that the author is not engaging in the rendering of legal, financial, or professional advice. The content within this book has been derived from various sources. Please consult a licensed professional before attempting any techniques outlined in this book.

Investing in property can be a risky business, just like any other investment. Historical growth in property prices does not necessarily mean that prices will increase in the future.

A property may be repossessed if you do not keep up the payments on its mortgage. It is important that you are aware of the terms and conditions set out in the lender's mortgage offer.

No warranties of any kind are declared or implied.

By reading this document, the reader agrees that under no circumstances is the author responsible for any losses, direct or indirect, which are incurred as a result of the use of the information contained within this document, including, but not limited to, errors, omissions, or inaccuracies.

It is important that you carry out your own due diligence on all property transactions, partnerships, joint ventures, lenders, and conditions.

You need to know and become comfortable with your own level of risk. Some people are very risk-averse, and others are gung-ho in their actions. This book aims to give you the knowledge, courage, and confidence you need to make your own decisions to acquire property. Please do not become a motivated buyer for the wrong reasons.

This book covers acquiring property in England. The other UK nations of Scotland, Wales, and Northern Ireland have their own devolved government that can and do make their own rules. These, in some cases, will differ from England. That said, there are often ways to make an idea or principle work in a slightly different format.

The above is the scary bit that must be noted by all readers of this book. Investing in property can be very lucrative if you know what you are doing. This book will undoubtedly get you thinking and, hopefully, into "your OWN property".

Contents

Foreword	XI
Dedication	XV
Unlock Your Potential (FREE download)	XVI
Introduction	XVII
Let's start at the beginning	XIX
Understanding OWN	XXV
Visualise OWN	XXIX
Section 1: OPPORTUNITY	1
1. Wasted Money	3
2. Find Sellers, Not Property	9
3. Become Mortgage Ready	19
Section 2: WIZARDRY	37
4. Think Differently	39
5. Acquiring Property	45
6. Finding Deposit Money	69
Section 3: NURTURE	77

7.	Adding Value	79
8.	Your Property Ladder	83
9.	Property Buying Bonus	87
Your Next Steps		91
My Power Team		95
Discovery Days		96
Acknowledgements		98

Foreword

I first met Andy Haynes early in 2009 when he invited me to speak at his own property networking event. That was when the banks and the economy crashed, and property prices were in freefall.

For many people, it was a challenging time to be investing in the property market. It was common for investors who didn't know what they were doing to lose everything.

Andy was very, *very* different from them, and I was immediately struck by his tenacity to find a way to save (at that time) his small property portfolio. There was no way he would have given up on his hard work.

In 2003, I founded the Property Investor's Network for serious property investors, and I invited Andy to join in with other delegates on my 12-month Property Mastermind Programme, where I offer them a target of achieving a £1,000,000 property portfolio plus a £50,000 annual income.

It was an excellent decision for Andy because within 12 months, he had risen to my challenge and achieved a very sizeable portfolio which meant he was in a position to replace his work salary. Not bad in a falling market!

Andy decided to go part-time in his day job - he loved working there too much to give it up entirely (at that time) - and I invited him to work with me, training others to achieve their own financial freedom.

Since then, we have both separately built multi-million-pound portfolios and inspired thousands of investor students to become property millionaires by building their own portfolios. This has given them a choice for what age they retire and the lifestyle they want to lead.

This all starts with acquiring your very first property, and this book, **No More Rent**, could be the catalyst you need to follow your own dream. The book is split into three sections, each taking you on a journey to provide you with the knowledge you need to get started. These strategies, used correctly, absolutely work.

Who knows... maybe you'll catch the property investing bug just like I (and Andy) did, and you will want to have your own portfolio. If you do, I might just know someone who can help you...

I always say that investing in property is one of the best investments you can make... second only to investing in yourself. In buying this book, you have already demonstrated you have planted that property seed. Now allow it to germinate and grow.

Simon Zutshi

Author Property Magic

This book is dedicated to YOU (the reader) for having the dream of owning your own home and having the courage to do something about it... think differently and be inspired!

FREE GIFT FOR YOU
download your 8-page guide

DISCOVER HOW TO...

1. CONQUER YOUR FEAR
2. MANAGE YOUR TIME
3. PREVENT PROCRASTINATION
4. BECOME MORE OPEN-MINDED
5. DREAM BIGGER

AND UNLOCK YOUR POTENTIAL...

MASTER PLAN FOCUS

Introduction

I was 23 years old when I was lucky (or wise) enough to buy my first house.

Property was selling like the proverbial "hot cakes" back then and prices were going up and up. When my daughter was born, shortly after I moved into this house, I remember thinking that she would surely really struggle to buy her own place in twenty years if house price growth continued as it was.

My creative plan was to immediately see if I could buy a second home that I could give to her when she came of age. I went down to a Building Society and was flatly refused! You were not allowed to have two residential mortgages and they had not heard of Buy to Let mortgages, as they hadn't been created. These were introduced in 1996, some 12 years after I had the idea. I entered the Buy to Let mortgage market, initially by accident in 1997, and then I began to get serious in my portfolio acquisition from 2002 onwards.

By the way, when the time came, I didn't actually give one of my houses to my daughter - instead, she bought it at a very favourable price, but instead in 2015 when she was aged 30.

Her age was a realisation to me that the ages of first-time house buyers were becoming higher. I think today it's about 39 years old, and I want to do something positive to bring this average age back into people's twenties.

This book aims to provide the belief to first-time buyers that they can make this happen.

Let's start at the beginning

You might be one of the numerous people who say "property prices are too expensive" and if you do, I agree with you. As far back as I can remember in my property-buying years, this exact phrase has been said by so many, and it will continue to be the same in the future too.

My name is Andy Haynes, and I'm the author of this book.

I bought my very first residential house for my family to live in back in 1983. It cost SO MUCH MONEY to buy, and I needed to decide quickly because others were queuing up to take it. Fortunately, the widow who was selling her house took a liking to me, and she made sure it would become ours.

LESSON ONE: *"People buy from (and sell to) people"*

Always remember that anything and everything in life usually revolves around a relationship. It's how you communicate with others that is key to many things. Your success in buying a property will be strongly influenced by how well you get on with people because people buy from (and sell to) people.

You may be thinking that you've fallen at the first hurdle as you are NOT a people person. If this is the case, all is not lost. Please stick with it as there are some easy things to do - even if it's just for a temporary period of time - that will endear you to others.

The first house I bought was a 3-bed semi-detached with a garage and garden in the riverside Georgian town of Bewdley. I paid £23,750 for it. Now in 2023, it's probably worth £275,000 (there's more about the capital appreciation of houses in Chapter 1, so I'll come back to the significance of this house price increase).

I needed to find £24,000, or thereabouts, as there are other costs involved in buying a house (again, more on this later), and I agree that this looks so cheap compared to its value today. However, back in 1983, I remember so well my uncle saying to me how high-priced my new house was, in his opinion. He was basing his rationale on the fact that he and his wife had bought a (similar) family home a generation earlier for just £5,000 (and they thought that was costly at the time).

Looking back, I don't know how I afforded it… but I knew I needed to. I remember that feeling of paying out money to landlords, month after month, year after year. At first, I was very grateful to them for allowing me to have my own place away from my parents, but I did see it as paying the mortgage on someone else's property.

What if I could find a way to have no more wasted rent money and buy my own place?

My will to make this happen was so strong that it had to happen. Nothing was going to stop me, even though on paper, my financial circumstances didn't look very good.

LESSON TWO: *"There is always a solution to have the things you TRULY need"*

There is a huge difference between wanting something and needing it. A 'want' is a wish, whilst a 'need' is essential. It becomes more definite and, in turn, has a clarity of focus. It is much easier to do things outside of your comfort zone when the prize for doing so is very much worth the price.

Later on in this book, I'm going to share with you ideas that will make you think. Perhaps it will be easier to walk away than to do what it takes. I'm just planting a seed here for you: think about your own personal urgency and be ready to accept and adopt new ways of thinking to acquire your OWN property.

In 1983 I was in my early 20's, just married, and needed to put firm roots down. Until this point, I had rented various flats and houses, and I know exactly how it feels when the landlord tells you the rent is going up, or they want the house back in order to sell. You find yourself constantly being on the lookout for your next place.

On the other hand, my own home that I was now buying gave me peace of mind that no one could evict my family and me on a whim (except for maybe the mortgage lender if I didn't keep up my payments - but I was determined that would never happen).

My property investing happened by chance after becoming an accidental landlord. My wife spotted a house in the countryside (at a purchase price we couldn't afford back then) that was also up for rent. I did a little homework on prices and realised I could rent out our own house for more than the cost of the rent on the new potential one (after negotiating), which was situated on the edge of a farm. It meant we could live where we wanted and still have a foot on the property ladder.

It was years later when the 'penny dropped' for me... what if I could buy a second property and rent that out for a profit too? You see, at this time I was working at the BBC: I had a great job, reasonable pay (although you always need more, eh?), brilliant prospects, along with the chance of contributing to a final salary pension. The challenge came when my independent financial advisor (IFA) explained that I needed to put in much more money each month than I already was to be able to retire at the income level I required.

Paying extra into my pension was definitely NOT an option. You know how it is, household bills, family expenses, mortgage, car (insurance, tax, MOT, and fuel). There's never usually any cash left over at the end of the month.

I asked myself: "What would need to happen to get myself another rental property?" If I could just scrape together enough for a deposit and find a great tenant, I knew that my initial money down would be returned to me over time through the rental profit. And if I could then maybe get another property in a similar way, it would add to my income for retirement. It was a great plan... and I made it happen.

If I had to do this all over again, I know that with my current knowledge and experience, along with the skills and techniques I'm going to share with you in this book, I would be able to grow my portfolio much faster, and need far less of my own money - maybe even none of my own money!

Now, 40 years after buying that first house, I own a £multi-million property portfolio and, to be clear, I'm not telling you this to boast or impress you. My intention is simply to inspire you to know that if I can do it, you can too. I have used the very same ways that I will be sharing with you in this book to build that portfolio. It is possible if you dream big enough and take action.

It all starts first with getting your **OWN** property.

ANDY HAYNES

Understanding OWN

This book is split into three sections and each of these has a specific direction for you to follow when selecting, acquiring, and enhancing your OWN property.

OWN is an acronym for Opportunity, Wizardry, and Nurture, and there is a reason for naming them using these words. Let's look at the reasoning behind each section in turn:

OPPORTUNITY

'You get what you are looking for' is a phrase I'm sure you have already come across. Some of us believe it to be true and others just put things down to luck. However, we all have a Reticular Activation System (RAS) inside of us. It is said that if you focus hard on your goals, in other words, you "set your intent", your RAS will find for you the opportunities you are looking for.

Let me give you an example that I have experienced, and maybe you have too. Yours may not be the same item as mine but, all the same, I think you will know what I am talking about.

It was time for me to change my car, and I put some thought into choosing the make, model, and colour. As soon as I had done this, as if by magic, I started seeing exactly the same vehicle, on the roads, in car parks. In fact, it seemed like everywhere. The point is these cars had been there all the time, but I wasn't noticing them because that was not my focus. Now that it was, I easily recognised them.

The ways I am going to share with you about finding your OWN property will become easier if you adopt this RAS approach.

In this section, I will also help you with the process of finding and buying a property. If you have never been through this process before, it can be very daunting. There's so much to think about, including: how to deal with estate agents, making offers, mortgage brokers, surveyors, and solicitors, to name just a few.

WIZARDRY

You may think this is an unusual word to have selected for naming this section. It's been deliberately chosen, though.

There's a sense of magic in what I will be revealing to you later on. Please don't skip ahead, there is an order which has been chosen to tell you about each step.

I don't know if you like to be entertained by magicians. I personally find them fascinating. Every time I watch a trick being performed, I am amazed and cannot help but wonder how it was done. On the surface, the performers have practised and trained themselves to deliver 'fascination' every time, and yet, behind the scenes, there is a set way or procedure that needs to be followed in the background to deliver the result.

The art of magic can be ruined when you know exactly how it was performed. You cannot then help but notice what's going on - those previously hidden secrets - when you are in the know. The property investing techniques I am going to share with you might seem a little bit like a magic trick after the previously unseen methods have been shown to you. You may even think "Is that it?" I hope you do... because then I will know that I have easily explained the process and what needs to be done.

You don't know what you don't know... and I want to let you in on the ways successful property investors are using to build their portfolio, and you can use them too to get your first property.

NURTURE

Acquiring your property is not the end of it. There is a lot more that you need to do in order to enhance your investment and maximise your profit.

This section highlights ways to quickly add value to your property and build your equity. Equity is the difference between what the property value has now become, minus what you originally bought it for. It is also known as your net worth.

There are also further ways you can help yourself, along with your mindset, to acquire further properties and grow your portfolio, if this is what you want to do. This book can help you to get started.

There are also other ways I can support you in the future, if and when you are ready.

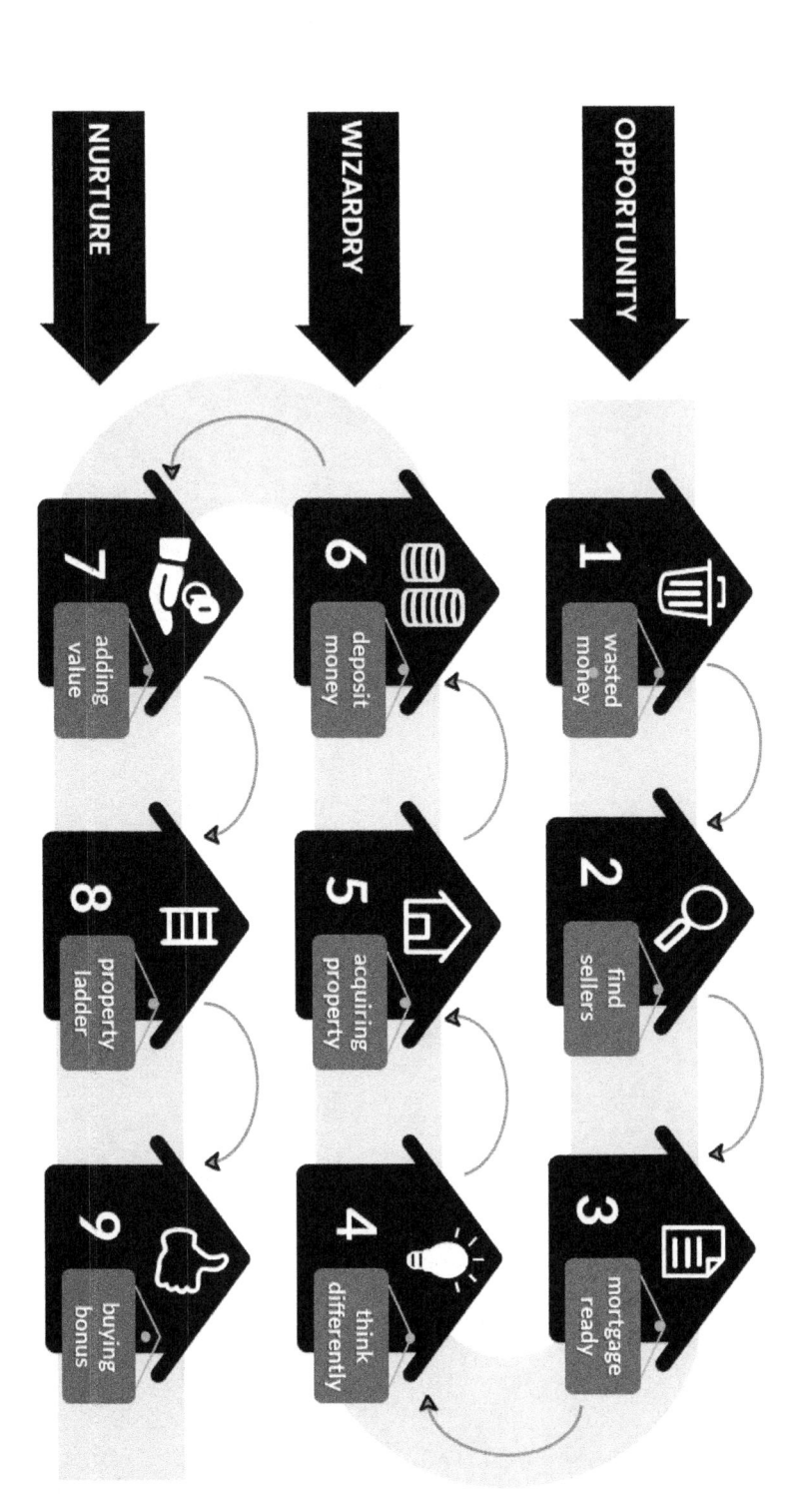

OPPORTUNITY

1. wasted money
2. find sellers
3. mortgage ready

WIZARDRY

4. think differently
5. acquiring property
6. deposit money

NURTURE

7. adding value
8. property ladder
9. buying bonus

Section 1: OPPORTUNITY

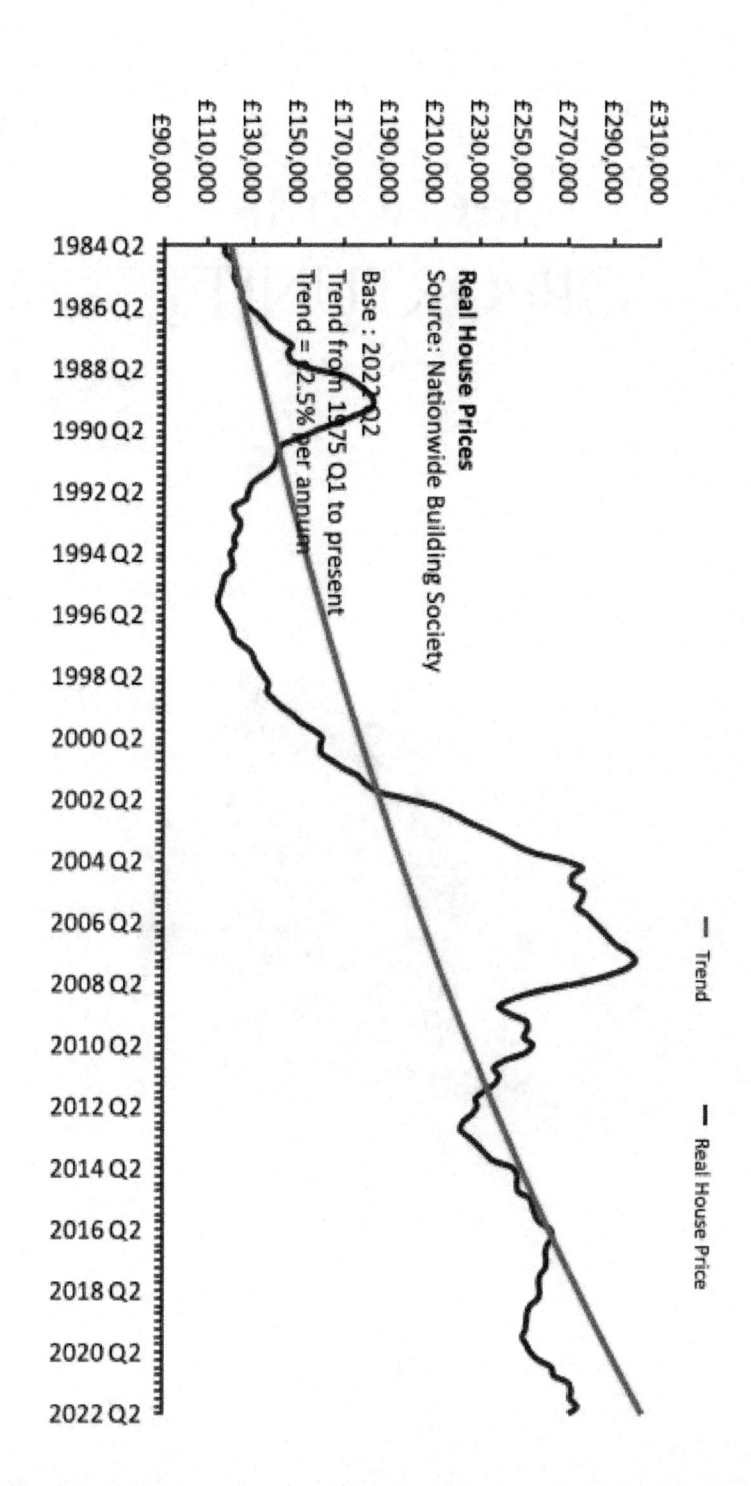

Real House Prices
Source: Nationwide Building Society

Base : 2022 Q2
Trend from 1975 Q1 to present
Trend = 2.5% per annum

One

Wasted Money

Property prices in the UK are cyclical and over time they go up and they come down in value. This is usually driven by inflation and recession, along with supply and demand.

It's been reported online that the UK government needs to build 300,000 new homes each year and this target is not being met. When you include the fact that the UK has an increasing population it means there is an undersupply of homes.

So over time, there is a general upward trend in home prices and you will notice in the illustration on page 2 that it shows them doubling on average every 7 years. There is no knowing what will happen to property prices in the future - however, history does leave clues.

Many 18-40 year-olds have been priced out of the property market, feeling they are unable to buy, so instead have to pay a high proportion of their income on rent. This is a daunting reality and there is now a widespread and growing group who face the prospect of being the generation who will always need to rent their home.

The media, their peers, and a seemingly diminishing bank balance all provide evidence that it will never be possible, and I suspect there is a growing cohort of the British population who have already made up their minds that they will never be able to purchase their own home.

This (understandable) mindset, when you compound it with the fact there is safety and comfort in numbers, leads to people feeling a huge amount of bonding from being part of a herd who are just like them. This means it becomes really difficult to go in the opposite direction, to break the norm and be different, especially if you are put under pressure.

Maybe this book can offer you the necessary courage to take back your dreams and vision, as an individual, to make your property ownership a reality. Norman Vincent Peale, who is said to be the father of positive thinking, is well known for the following quote: "Change your thoughts and you change your world".

LESSON THREE: *Conduct the orchestra, rather than just playing in it*

Everyone has an opinion on things and this is absolutely their right. The trouble is, those who are the louder or more influential in society tend to drown out the less brave. It's much simpler at times to go with the flow and not rock the boat. It is often said, "To change your life, you have to change your life", and this means doing things outside of your present comfort zone. This is where your personal growth comes from and it is well worth finding the necessary courage.

If you find yourself a lone voice in your desire to buy your own place, reach out so that my team and I can help you. You will find resources to help you at the end of this book. In the meantime, please keep reading as I want to inspire you even further with why you should and how you can.

Should you stay renting?

Living in a property, regardless of whether you are renting or buying is very similar. However, there is a world of difference, mostly at a subconscious level, that goes on inside of us as people. It's the same thought process (or feeling) whether we are talking about cars, laptops, property, or anything else you can choose to rent or buy.

If that item or possession is truly yours, you value it more, look after it better, and it generally lasts longer. Something that you pay to rent (or lease) is just a tool to be used, it doesn't belong to you in the same way and is purely a means to an end.

You can still love something that is either bought or leased but the item that is not really yours is not thought of the same, in many cases.

For me, driving a company car was a different feeling from when I bought my own, improving a property that wasn't mine didn't always happen if left up to me, and depending on what repairs or maintenance issues had arisen, it dictated whether I got my landlord in to fix it or not. This resulted in the property becoming more tired.

If major things happened, like a boiler breakdown, kitchen door hinge breaking, leaks, etc., it was nice not needing to pay and having the landlord arrange and fund these repairs.

Depending on which side of the fence you want to pick, there are pros and cons to both buying and renting. If you like having the free reign to move more easily into a new place or different city, or like having the peace of mind of no major property expenses, or even living in a property you couldn't afford to buy, renting is definitely for you.

On the other hand, you are paying out rent with no financial gain and it feels like wasted money, there's no potential increase in property values to benefit from over the long term, and often a mortgage payment is less per month than the rent.

You will already know which side of the buying or renting argument you want to defend, and I am guessing that by choosing to read this book, you are looking for ways to buy and acquire your own property.

The general rule of thumb is that you should invest in assets that appreciate in value and lease the items that depreciate. As an example, this means buying property, antiques, and gold bonds, and instead renting cars, computers, and mobile phones. Of course, these lists of assets and liabilities are not exhaustive and there are many other things you can, and should, include.

Shift in thinking

I may be totally wrong on this but I feel there is a whole (and growing) generation of people who are already of the mindset that they could never be in the position of buying their own place to live. Most media outlets, peer groups, and housing charities seem to fuel this belief.

This book intends to help you to begin to think and act differently. It will stretch your thinking - big time! You may feel its ideas are not plausible or possible, and that is okay to a certain extent, BUT I encourage you to keep an open mind. The strategies discussed in a later chapter do work and I have evidence to prove it as I have personally used many of these tactics.

It takes courage to do things outside of your comfort zone, it's hard sometimes going against the crowd, especially when loved ones start to tell you you're misguided, being brainwashed, and will "lose the shirt off your back". I know this because it happened to me. My parents were so protective of me. It takes a lot of guts to carry on, regardless.

LESSON FOUR: Jealousy wrapped in the clothes of a guardian

Often your friends, family, and work colleagues will not mind you succeeding, just so long as you are not doing better than them. When this happens (or they think it is about to happen) they start pulling you back, telling you that you are wrong, filling your mind with what-ifs that will scare you and maybe put you off.

Please recognise the signs of this occurring. Stay resolute and follow your own heart. There will more than likely become a point in the future where they come back to you and ask you to show them how you achieved and succeeded. This is a lovely feeling when you experience it.

It can be done. It takes belief. It takes tenacity. Things will never change if things never change. Become the person who breaks the mould and achieves your goals and dreams. Have the courage of your convictions.

Successful people are decisive. Allow this book to be your catalyst for that change.

Two

Find Sellers, Not Property

Properties come in all sorts of shapes, sizes, designs, and locations. You may already have your preferences on all of these. That is great, except... be prepared for your first house to simply become a stepping stone toward your ideal place. It might take two or three house moves to get to your forever home.

LESSON FIVE: *Think differently from many other house buyers*

Many people have their dream home in mind. They have collected bits of furniture, sometimes family heirlooms, and in their head, they can see exactly the property where it will all fit very nicely. House hunters look around a property and are immediately put off if it is not perfect from day one when they move in. You might currently think like these people.

The bargain, where you can make money, is to acquire places that look jaded, maybe un-loved, tired, old-fashioned, and (dare I say) ugly. These are the buildings you can transform into a "beautiful swan" and build yourself equity.

Properties are also referred to by many names. I think these have been used as a marketing ploy over the years to make them seem more expensive. The common property types are flats, terraced, semi-detached, detached, and bungalows, where you would assume a terraced house to be less valuable than, say, a detached house. So, you will see these terraced places referred to as townhouses or mews properties, and flats referred to as apartments.

Buildings will be freehold or leasehold. Generally, a house is freehold, while a flat is leasehold. I will explain why in just a few moments. However, occasionally a flat can be freehold (usually if it's in a smaller block of perhaps two flats), and houses can be leasehold. In fact, there was a trend by some new house builders to sell their brand new houses as leaseholds because, over the years, it could become very lucrative. This loophole has now been stopped, and I'm just making you aware in case you come across some relatively newer houses being leasehold.

A freehold building is where the purchaser owns all of the building and the land it sits on, including the garden, garage, etc., as shown on its title at the Land Registry. You also own the air space above your building and land.

A leasehold property is a place where you rent the building from a person or business who owns the freehold. Typical leasehold lengths (from new) are 99, 125, or 999 years.

Picture a building containing eight apartments. The person owning the middle one (with other flats above, below, or even to the side) will only usually have control and responsibility from their floor to their ceiling and between the walls of the flat unit. The extent of their responsibility (including other terms and conditions) will be detailed in the Head Lease given to them by the freeholder.

A leasehold property normally has shared parts of the building which, from time to time, require maintenance and upkeep. This can include painting the hallways and staircases, cutting lawns and other gardening, and fixing the roof or other parts of the building. A lot of this can be covered by an insurance policy or with a service-level agreement. However, the leaseholders have a share of those costs to pay, called Service Charges. They are commonly paid monthly but can be quarterly, every six months, or even yearly, and are paid to the freeholder. Often a freeholder will outsource this responsibility to a Managing Agent, and there could be a further charge to cover the agent's services.

LESSON SIX: *Not all properties are registered at Land Registry*

It is much easier if they are as there is a digital record (available online for a small fee) showing the extent of the land and building(s) footprint. However, before (approximately) the year 2000, there may be properties not shown on the government Land Registry website.

These are older properties not sold and bought in the 21st century because if they were, the buying and selling process would mean a solicitor preparing the documentation for inclusion online at Land Registry.

Be careful when going online and searching for the land registry information. There are websites that offer the services of providing you with a property title and plan - and they look very authoritative like the government website - but they can charge their own fee, and this is often much more than from the official government Land Registry website.

In my experience, houses tend to have better capital growth than flats, and by this, I mean they tend to increase in value better. Of course, this is a generalisation, there are certain cities like London where most properties that people live in are flats. However, this is not so in other parts of the UK, and I have found that my personal houses have given me greater equity than the apartments I own. Indeed, I have sold off some of my original apartments to use their equity in what I consider to be better property investments. To be clear, I'm not saying never to buy a flat, I just want you to know that, in my opinion, a house will probably increase in value at a greater rate.

A property is worth what someone is prepared to pay for it. Prices will fluctuate through popularity, along with supply and demand situations. That value will often be checked by a surveyor, especially if you are asking a mortgage lender to fund your purchase. These surveyors base their approval on other similar properties in the area, which are referred to as comparable properties. The surveyor will also take into account the condition of the property, compared with other similar ones.

I am going to explain how to acquire property in part two of this book. Before I do that, I want to help you begin thinking differently. Remember, the first home you buy doesn't have to be the best; you can move and upgrade once you are on the property ladder.

Another thing to consider is... it will be your purchase, but could you share that space with other people, friends, work colleagues, or other lodgers? Before you shout a definitive "no," there are many financial benefits to doing just this!

Keep in mind we are talking here about getting your first home... it is simply that stepping stone or a phase in your property journey. Having others to live with you (and I don't mean a life or relationship partner - although it could be) will assist you in affording the property. I know about people who have done just this. Their house with others paying rent which covers the bills. In their case, they covered all of the utilities and their monthly mortgage payment, meaning they didn't need anything taken from their own income. In fact, the government makes this an attractive thing to do as (at the time of writing) they currently have a Rent a Room Scheme which allows you a tax-free rental income of up to £7,500.00 a year.

The next way I want to ask you to be open-minded is to look for sellers and not the property. See things with a new way of thinking.

I, probably like you, use online property portals to scour what is for sale on the open market. My favourite go-to place is Rightmove, although you could use Zoopla, On The Market, or other property portals.

Before I tell you what to look out for, think briefly about what you have done up until now. I am sure you will have selected an area, put in your price range, the number of bedrooms you would prefer, and pressed 'search'. Then you scan the images looking for places you like the look of and then read the price and description. That is how most people use online property portals.

The way to find property bargains is to go about things differently, and I want to draw your attention to think more about the picture, the estate agent, and the description.

If there is no picture shown, up until now, you would have just scrolled past to look at the next property. This is a normal habit for people. Just imagine though, if that was your property that you need to sell and it is simply being passed by with no interest. No inquiries, no viewings, no sale. How would you feel? There are two general reasons for no photos. The first is the estate agent hasn't yet taken and/or uploaded them online (very unlikely). Secondly, the state of the property means photos would not attract buyers. Most people searching want to have the perfect property to move straight into and not have to do any work.

I have invited you to think differently. How motivated - you might even say desperate - could these sellers be? If you know the price will reflect the property's condition and you can get a bargain, might this tempt you to love finding a property with no, or maybe just one very carefully taken image?

Next, look at the selling agent. You will probably recognise the popular estate agents in an area but look for the ones which are not local. There are several national agents that are used because of their low fees and/or simplicity. Some names of these agents, which I see regularly, are Express Estate Agents, Springbok, and Get-an-Offer. I am not suggesting there is anything wrong with these agencies. They could simply indicate the circumstances and mood of the seller in wanting a quick sale.

An out-of-town agent is not going to travel miles to show you around a property. This can be good news as it means the viewing is likely to be carried out by the owner. This is great because everything happens as a result of relationships (whether business or personal) between people. If you can interact well with others, see things from their point of view, understand their needs, and help to find the right solution for them, things align for a truly ethical win/win outcome.

Also, notice if the same property is offered for sale with more than one agent. I have noticed some with three agent boards, and this gives an indication of "I don't care which agent sells it, just so long as one of them does"!

Another tell-tale sign is in reading the property description. Some of these are so basic it does not tell you anything or everything that a prospective buyer would want to know. It might list the property rooms but gives no dimensions. Words such as "priced to sell fast", "no onward chain", "reduced for a fast sale", and "all offers considered" also give a good indication that some sort of negotiation on the purchase price and/or terms is possible.

Properties that have been on the market for a long time are good to research, too. People could become more motivated for a sale the longer their place is not sold. Most property portals allow you to change the order of a list, arranging it by price or newest on the market. Conversely, the bottom of this latter list shows those which have been for sale the longest. Another giveaway is an out-of-season photo, such as snow shown in the middle of summer or certain flowers in full bloom when they shouldn't be.

This next tip I will share with you is a biggy! Since finding this piece of software, it has allowed me to be much more knowledgeable when speaking with potential sellers. I am also delighted to tell you that you can (at the time of writing) use it for free. There is a paid-for upgrade available. The no-cost version works just fine, though. It is an extension available to use on the Chrome search engine when you are using Rightmove. It is called PaTMa which I believe stands for Property and Tenant Manager. This plug-in extension, when set up correctly, will show you the history of a property up for sale with certain estate agents. It details when it first went on the market, if it has been sold and then returned to the market, and any price increases or decreases. I find it really useful, and I think you will agree too.

You must see things from the seller's position, put yourself in their shoes, assume how they might be feeling, and it will give you an indication of their position and motivation.

Also, notice properties that are both for sale and to let. There is a very good reason for doing so, which I will explain in greater detail in Part Two of this book.

When you come across a property that you think has great potential, it is very important to take action immediately to see if it is a deal for both the seller and you. If you think about things for too long, you will miss out. This often happens when you allow fear to paralyse you and you over-analyse to see if the deal is as good as you initially thought it was, and then you talk yourself out of doing it, or someone else nabs your bargain.

This is very common, and I am deliberately pointing it out to you because I want you to recognise the signs in your behaviour. It does require courage to work through Part Two, and being forewarned will help to start and form your necessary attitude.

There are opportunities everywhere, and these opportunities are never lost, they are found by someone else. This last sentence is something to remember firmly, so you benefit instead of others.

Three

Become Mortgage Ready

Before we get started on the road to you acquiring your first property, there are some essential things you need to know about yourself first.

What I am about to explain will be different for every individual, albeit some of us will be similar. This chapter is also important if you plan on working with others to buy a property, maybe a friend or relationship partner, as they will influence your ability and affect their outcome.

You need to be absolutely honest with yourself and your situation. There can be no financial skeletons in your cupboard of which you are unaware. It is not the end of the world if you are not "squeaky clean" with your credit rating, as there are some workarounds.

If you intend to get a mortgage, you must know that your credit rating is at a suitable level. In the UK, four leading credit reference agencies know an awful lot about everyone as individuals, influencing financial decisions made at a particular moment in time. These four are Equifax, Experian, TransUnion, and Crediva.

Different lenders, such as mortgage providers, car loans, bank loans, phone companies, credit card lenders, etc., as well as landlords, and employers, all usually use at least one of these agencies. Some will use just one, others potentially all of them. This is important because if you have a problem shown with one agency, your mortgage broker may be able to use a lender that uses the services of one of the other agencies.

You can find out what agencies know about you by paying each of them a monthly subscription. Alternatively, some companies show results from all four agencies for a single subscription. You can find your preferred credit score service online, and a company I have used is: CheckMyFile.co.uk

You will be amazed at the level of detail they know about you - I know I was astounded when I first looked. It did, though, make me look differently into how I did everything to do with money and who I was associated with financially.

They know how many credit cards you have, and if you pay in full or make the minimum monthly payment amount, they can show any correctly paid and missed payments on any of your borrowings. They see any bank accounts and know if you use your overdraft, and - very important for you - they see other people you are linked with in bank accounts and mortgages, etc., and these links mean you are rated by the other person's financial status. So, your situation will likely be affected if they have financial problems.

It is well worth you checking your personal file to see your current position, and I think having them update you every month is beneficial. It is easy for a missed payment to happen, and you should be in the know to correct it straightaway if you can.

With many lenders, credit cards with outstanding amounts each month, and any personal loans will affect how much mortgage they will lend you. A typical lender might offer you up to 4.5 times your annual salary for a mortgage amount. (Note: this multiplier can vary with your circumstances, and from time to time). So, let's say you earn £30,000 a year; this could indicate a mortgage loan of £135,000. However, if you have money outstanding in personal loans or on credit cards, this generally gets deducted from your annual salary before the multiplier is used. So, if there is £10,000 on credit cards and a £12,000 personal loan, you have just £8,000 x 4.5 for a mortgage amount of £36,000 which is probably not going to buy you a property.

So, get yourself mortgage-ready by paying off personal loans, clearing overdrafts, and getting rid of credit card debt. I realise this is easier said than done, but it is likely to be necessary if you really want a mortgage. Pay things on time and demonstrate you are paying something back, not just servicing the debt.

When I understood this, I changed my spending habits by using my credit cards less and paying off the most expensive interest loan

I had first. Then when it had been paid back, I used that amount of money to pay on top of the next credit card payment, so I was overpaying as much as possible, and so on for the next debt until I had finally cleaned the slate.

It wasn't always easy, but it soon felt terrific and became an addiction to be free of those loans. It's incredible how you can change your thinking when you truly put your mind to things. If you are in a relationship, you also need your partner onboard, compounding the speed it takes to have zero outstanding debt.

Another critical factor in getting yourself mortgage-ready is to make sure you are included on the Electoral Register. Lenders put a lot of weight on their decision of whether to lend or not based on this one thing. They like to go back at least three years to check you have been living where you say you have, and they want to see the clear evidence.

MORTGAGES

There are many mortgage brokers to choose from, but I am now very cautious about who I trust to look after this crucial area. Some brokers are tied to using specific companies, but you want an independent broker with access to the products across the whole market.

Early in my property investing journey, I selected a broker for a great reason - albeit, it soon became clear I was wrong to pick them because I later found out their knowledge was very limited. If you would like help choosing a broker to help you, I have included some in my Power Team list, which is available to you as a complimentary download using the QR code and web link towards the front of this book.

Mortgage lenders range from those you know on most high streets, to companies you've probably never heard of before. They all have their quirks, and your broker should help you select the best fit for your needs. There are mortgage products for most British citizens, foreign nationals, and ex-pats.

Some people make a major error in selecting a mortgage based solely on the monthly payment. Products can also include arrangement fees and other costs, which can significantly increase the amount you pay. I know that a lower mortgage payment will look attractive, but I just want to make you aware that other factors should be taken into consideration.

LESSON SEVEN: *Should you choose a free broker or pay them a fee?*

I think you would agree that many people are drawn toward the attractiveness of not having to pay a mortgage broker for their services. I was just like this at first. Nowadays, I deliberately pay my broker a fee for their work.

Every business needs to make money to cover its costs and pay its wages. Your broker will be given a commission directly from the lender, and this is why a few do not have to charge you for their work.

Human nature dictates they might select the best product for their needs rather than yours.

For this reason, I want my broker to have a fee paid by me and not be influenced by their commission. Yes, they will still be paid by the lender, but I have received a better, unbiased service from brokers I have paid myself.

There are two main mortgage types: interest only or repayment. With an interest-only loan, as the name suggests, you only pay the agreed interest amount, which means the full loan amount remains outstanding. You will need to demonstrate a payment mechanism to repay the balance at the end of your mortgage term.

Initially, on my home mortgage, I took the interest-free route because I knew I could sell some of my property portfolio at the appropriate time to pay off my mortgage. If (unlike me) you are only going to buy one property – the one you live in (even if you sell it and buy another) – I believe you should take out a repayment mortgage.

The length of a mortgage term will vary on quite a few factors, such as your age, the marketplace at any particular time, and the chosen lender. Typically you could get a 25, 30, or even 40-year mortgage term. My lender gave me a mortgage up to my 70th birthday. There are other companies, I believe, that will allow a higher age.

The other type of mortgage is a repayment one. This is where your monthly payment will include an element of interest and the amount of the mortgage (capital) that you borrowed. This means your monthly payments will be higher, but you will have paid back all of the loan, including the interest, by the end of the agreed term.

This repayment scheme method is not equal amounts of capital and interest every month. At the beginning of the term, it will consist of mostly interest and little capital, and then towards the end of the term, this payment is mainly capital repaid and a smaller amount of interest.

For this reason, if your first home is merely a stepping stone, you might consider taking out an interest-only mortgage to lower your monthly outgoings. Then, when you move to a property that you are planning to live in for much longer, you could take out a repayment mortgage. This is the route I chose when I bought my first residential property.

I changed my mortgage to become a repayment one when I had just eight years left before it needed clearing. This was because I had decided not to sell off certain other properties as originally planned, and this meant that I had a fairly hefty monthly payment to find as there were only 96 payments available to pay it off. However, because the value of the property had risen significantly since I had bought it, the loan to value was very low which meant I received a favourable mortgage rate, reducing my monthly payment, which was a bonus.

You might not get a choice to select between the two types of mortgage. It does depend on the state of the marketplace at any particular time. Residential mortgage lenders prefer you to take a repayment mortgage. I think this could be seen as having a duty of care to their borrowers to ensure the full amount owed can be repaid. If it was interest only, it might be the property has to be sold to repay the loan, and then where would you live if you no longer have your property?

If a property market continues to thrive and go up in value (which history has shown it to do over the long term), you may be in a position to sell, clear your interest-only balance in full, and use your equity to buy a lower priced property to suit your needs at that time.

I mentioned earlier about having credit card debt(s). Some lenders are okay with this and others will not allow it. Therefore, be honest and explain all of your circumstances to your chosen mortgage broker to allow them to suggest the best lender for you, at that time.

By the way - please don't keep chopping and changing mortgage brokers. I know this might be necessary if you and they are not getting on, but in the main, it's easier to stay with just the one who fully understands your position.

Mortgage brokers like to check you are mortgageable before 'wasting their time' with you and they will ask you if they can get you a mortgage Decision in Principle (referred to as a DIP). They tell you this is a good idea as it will be useful to show an estate agent or seller to show you are serious and in a position to proceed with a purchase.

I suggest you do not take this route. Firstly, you will know if you are likely to be able to get a mortgage by understanding your credit score, as talked about earlier in this book. Should you choose to do so (and you shouldn't feel obliged), you can show your credit file to your mortgage broker to show you are creditworthy. Secondly, every time a DIP is carried out, it will weaken the points you have on your credit score. As this goes down, lenders will think you are desperate and are trying many lenders for loans. They do not like to see this. Some DIPs are what they call a 'soft touch' and these do not affect your credit score. Your broker should advise you which type of DIP they are using.

From time to time, the government offer schemes to assist first-time buyers to get a mortgage. This has included Help To Buy, ISAs, and reduction or removal of Stamp Duty Land Tax (SDLT). These are very useful and can save you a lot of money, particularly by way of your deposit (to go along with your mortgage) towards the purchase. Search online for any available schemes suitable for your needs. They are regularly publicised.

Other ways to get onto the property ladder include a part share of a property. This is where you get a certain percentage share of a property, usually dependent on how much mortgage you are eligible to receive, and then you pay interest on the balance outstanding to the property owner. This is probably a Housing

Association. A part share might mean you initially own 25%, 50%, or 75% of the property. You can then buy further amounts of the property over time as and when you can re-mortgage or find other lump sums. I think a challenge with this scheme is that as property prices increase, so does the amount of money you need to find to buy a further share of your home.

SOLICITORS

When you buy or sell a property, you would use a conveyancing firm to complete the transaction. The cost for doing this normally depends on the buying or selling price and a law firm will give you a fixed price for doing their work. You may also have to pay HMRC tax if any Stamp Duty Land Tax (SDLT) is required. For first-time buyers (at the time of writing), there is a threshold of up to £425,000 where no SDLT is payable. Beyond this figure, there's a sliding scale rate and a tax calculator that you can find on the government's website. The threshold, though, is subject to change from time to time.

Conveyancing is the legal aspect of transferring ownership of property from the seller or vendor to the buyer. You hire a solicitor or licensed conveyancer firm to handle this process.

The conveyancing process involves your lawyer protecting your purchase at Land Registry. The parcel of land your property sits on is shown on a Title Plan, and the property itself has a Title Register which shows how much the property was purchased for, along with the date indicating when this happened. The register will also indicate if a charge or restriction has been placed against the Title.

A charge or restriction would show that a lender has secured their loan against the property, and they would remove it when you repay the loan. There can be a hierarchy of charges, called First Charge, Second Charge, and Third Charge, and this denotes the order in which the lenders are repaid. If not enough money is left, the lower-tier lenders may not receive anything after repaying the other charges.

There could be covenants showing on the registered title, indicating how the property and land can be used. A covenant is a bit like a set of rules for the property: for example, a caravan or van cannot be parked on the drive, or maybe the property can only be used as a dwelling and not for business use. There are many other types of covenants and your solicitor can advise you about these, should it be necessary.

The conveyancer will also carry out searches on the local area where the property sits. The types of searches necessary will vary around the UK, based on the local geography. So, if it's an existing or former mining area, searches showing the position of those mines and the mine shafts will need to be detailed to any mortgage lender. Other checks include investigating any plans, for example, a new road or railway line to be constructed close to the property. Also, the quality of the soil, flood planes, and the position of the property in relation to any dangerous substances, like a fuel depot, will be reported. There are many other searches and checks that could also be necessary. The timeframe for searches to be received back will vary and can be anywhere between two and six weeks. I have personally known it to take even longer in one particular case, but thankfully this was a one-off.

These checks might seem very scary. The idea is to make you aware of the condition of the local area so that you - and your mortgage lender - are informed and know the local environment.

You can also pay a surveyor to carry out a survey of any property. This is to tell you about the fabric, age, and condition of the premises. The report will advise you of any repairs (both major or minor) which could be necessary. Finding faults with a building might put you off. However, I see this as an opportunity to negotiate with the seller on the price and/or the terms of a possible purchase. For your peace of mind, you can also complete safety checks to tell you about the condition of the electrical wiring, drains, or gas appliances.

If you are using an estate agent, when your offer has been accepted by a seller or buyer, a form called a Memorandum of Sale (MOS) is used to detail the names of both sides of the transaction, along with the agreed terms, each side's chosen solicitor firms, and contact details. This MOS is then sent (or emailed) to all parties involved, including the conveyancers, so everyone involved is notified at the same time and clear on the arrangements. (In a later chapter in this book we will refer to a different document called a Heads of Terms (HoT) which is very similar to a MOS).

It's worth saying that at this stage, a solicitor or conveyancer can opt-out from representing a client. This can happen if they don't have the capacity to help at that time (in other words, they are too busy) or if there is a conflict of interest for them. A conflict of interest could mean that they are either currently representing, or have previously represented either you or the other side in another matter. Your legal team fully represents you as their client, and there should be no conversation (either verbally or in writing) with the opposite client. All matters during the transaction are referred to your or their chosen legal representative.

The buyer's lawyer will ask questions about the property to enable them to explain everything involved to you. These questions are referred to as 'Enquiries' and are sent over to the seller's solicitor for them to have answered by their client. The frequent questions would include simple things like who is responsible for each boundary, what is included in the sale (e.g. TV aerial, dustbins, plants, curtains, etc.) as well as more complex matters such as any known Right of Way across the land, and any known conflicts with neighbours, etc.

In readiness for a property sale, the conveyancer for the seller will prepare a contract that details all of the agreed transactions and selling/purchase price. After speaking with their respective clients, the lawyers on both sides agree upon a date to complete the transaction of both buying and selling the property. The completion date is usually one week after the exchange of contracts date and this period of time allows for the mortgage funds to be sent over to allow the transfer of agreed monies on the agreed completion date. It is possible, though not the norm, to both exchange contracts and complete the transaction on the same day, providing all parties involved are willing and all monies are in place to allow this to happen.

Your lawyer will not let you exchange contracts unless they have receipt of the money in their client account. They will also need a mortgage offer letter from your lender to prove all monies are available for the matter to complete. The moment of exchange of contracts makes the agreement legally binding and this means the seller must sell and the buyer has to buy. For this reason, if you are the purchaser, it would be sensible to make sure the property is insured from the point of exchange because if for example there was a fire, you would still need to go ahead with the transaction.

LESSON EIGHT: *Solicitor Client Account*

Your lawyer has the ability to set up a different kind of bank account and one that you and I as private individuals (or indeed as a normal business) are not eligible to hold. The funds in this account are ring-fenced for certain projects, matters, and transactions, and the money can only be used for those specific reasons.

These special bank accounts are scrutinised from time to time by the respective lawyer's regulator, and they must be an accurate reflection of their client's business matters. Monies cannot be borrowed from this account for any other purpose away from the intended use of why the money was placed in the account in the first place.

Your law firm will have a separate office bank account which they use to run their firm. Their fees for operating your matter can only be transferred from the client account into their office account after you give them permission to proceed.

There is an exception to what has just been explained, though, and that is by using an exchange with delayed completion, also known as an EDC.

It is normal to pay a 10% deposit (of the purchase price) at the time of exchange of contracts. This amount can be reduced or increased after negotiation between the buyer and seller. This money is forfeited by the purchaser should they not 'complete' at the agreed time, and the seller's lawyer will serve notice for the completion to go ahead. There are further penalties that the buyer becomes due to pay if completion does not happen on time.

Just before the completion happens, the lawyer will complete a bankruptcy check on the buyer, and no further charges or restrictions have been secured against the property Title whilst the matter has been going through the legal process.

The seller's solicitor must give a clear Title to the buyer – this means they will have to pay off any mortgage or other charge(s) against the property (previously secured by the seller) out of the sale proceeds. After all of the agreed deductions have been made, any balance from the funds will be paid over to the seller's chosen bank account.

The most often selected day of the week for completions to take place is on a Friday. I guess this gives the buyer the weekend to move into the property. It can be any day of the week, though, so long as it is not a designated bank holiday as funds will need to be sent from one solicitor's client account across to the other lawyer's client account. There can be a delay in the bank processing system and the transaction cannot go ahead until the funds have safely arrived into its destination bank account.

This completion day can be very fraught - picture yourself as the buyer, with all of your furniture and effects now in a removal firm's lorry, not able to access your new place and you not able or willing to unload it all again back into the place you have just left. Plus, if it's late on a Friday afternoon, it may mean nothing can move forward until the following Monday. Thinking through and carefully planning your completion day and date is a really useful thing to do.

Following completion, the respective legal teams will advise the Land Registry of the new owner's details and any mortgage lender's interest in a property. They will also pay any SDLT over to the government HMRC department, and then they will write to confirm everything has been processed, returning any due monies to you from their client account, held on your behalf.

The length of time it takes for this whole conveyancing process to happen will vary in every circumstance. As a guide, if everything goes smoothly (and it rarely does!) it can be around three months. So, it's not a super fast mechanism, and it can all fall apart at any point up until you have exchanged contracts. Should this happen, it means any money you have spent will normally be lost.

However, I feel that it's important to point out that this process can also go smoothly and quickly, so please don't be fearful. I asked you to remain open-minded at the beginning of this book, which includes being aware of any frustrating hiccups that might happen during processes such as this one. However, focusing on them and almost expecting them to happen won't assist this new mindset that you are working so hard on. Should any of the above hiccups arise, one of our Discovery Days can help to equip you with the knowledge that you need to work around them, calmly and efficiently. Details of our Discovery Days can be found at the back of this book.

For now, I look forward to seeing you in Section 2: WIZARDRY.

Section 2: WIZARDRY

Four

Think Differently

This is the section where you need to think differently about your own position and put yourself in the shoes of the seller. See things from their perspective. Understand their circumstances and know what they are going through. The reasons behind this should become clear throughout this chapter.

I will show you ways to find a property owner who is truly motivated to sell their house quickly, as opposed to a person who wants to sell but isn't in a hurry or concerned about the timescales.

You should look for **motivated sellers** for whom **speed and certainty** are important, which often means they will be flexible on the price and/or the terms.

A seller will put their property on the market, mostly for one of two reasons... (1) To release any profit (equity) or (2) To get rid of their mortgage debt.

The first group of people generally buy somewhere else, and the second group might move into a rented place. The point to note is that group two is not selling to make any money from the transaction. There is no (or very little) equity.

They could be in this position because the price of their property has fallen and when they have paid back their outstanding mortgage amount, there's no equity left, which means they will receive no money.

Here's an example: Let's say their property is worth £150,000 and their mortgage is £140,000. By the time they have paid their estate agent, solicitor, removal fees, etc., there will be none of the £10,000 equity left over. In fact, it might well cost them more, and they need to find money out of their own pocket just to get away from the property.

***LESSON NINE:** There are many reasons why an owner would be a motivated seller.*

Here are just a few:

Job relocation	Health reasons	Divorce
Broken chain	Emigration	Repossession
Bereavement	Redundancy	Retiring landlord
Clear debt	Mortgage arrears	Downsizing
Haunted house	School catchment	Move nearer family
Accidental landlord	Marriage	Expiring visa
Neighbourhood	Renovation needed	Rising mortgage
...and there are many more		

A seller in one (or more) of these motivated seller reasons wants to know they can move on in a guaranteed way and quickly, and because of these circumstances, this is why they will often be flexible on the price and/or the terms.

Only about 5% of sellers are truly motivated, which means most of the properties on the market are not the owners you will want to attract.

Many people find a property by using various property portals, such as Rightmove, Zoopla, On The Market, etc. This will take up loads of your time, albeit enjoyable if you like property and looking for a new home.

In Chapter 5, I will explain (a) how to use this searching time on portals wisely to spot the likely motivated seller properties and (b) ways you can use to provide the seller with the certainty they need.

Before we get there, firstly, I would like to help you with your mindset. I hope this is okay with you.

I would like you to open your mind to new ideas and possibly different ways of thinking. There are three blockers I often see:

1. An *'I know that already'* attitude

2. An *'I don't believe that'* mentality

3. A willingness to *allow distractions*

If you have maybe heard about what I will be explaining it's likely you will have already formed your opinion about it. This leads to closing your mind to the concepts which can be used.

I have been property investing for more than twenty years and have spoken with many, many, motivated sellers. I already know that the techniques that I am going to explain to you work extremely well.

That said, when I first learned about some of these methods, I found it hard to believe that anyone would want to sell me their property below market value. I now know, if the conditions suit, these sellers are delighted to get rid of their "problem property".

It will take a focus on your part to get things started as this is (probably) going to be outside of your comfort zone. It is not difficult. However, I wouldn't describe it as easy. There is definitely effort involved. The prize, though, can be well worth your effort - BIG TIME!

Secondly, I really believe in ethical investing and I strongly encourage you to have this same frame of mind.

A motivated seller might be emotional about their reason for getting rid of their home. Their property problem will not go away until they give up their property and they are looking for a way to come up with a workable solution. You may be able to help them, but please do not take advantage of them.

I have helped so many motivated sellers where the best outcome for them actually **wasn't** to sell me their property, even though I could have bought it well below market value. Instead, I worked with them to solve their challenges in a different way. There is plenty of opportunity to find a property for you to acquire, but with the owner being delighted that you are having their house at the same time.

Don't be greedy - it's best to find a solution that works for the seller first and then determine if it's also acceptable to you.

Although it can be for sad reasons that people need to move on, you will also need to remember that at the same time, it wasn't your fault they got into their predicament. You can be the answer (maybe even to their prayers) to allow them to see a way forward.

I have received so many hugs from motivated sellers who can now get on with the next chapter in their life, as a result of the solution that we made happen, together.

Selling (and indeed buying) property can be VERY stressful and this is another reason a motivated seller generally wants the whole process to take place quickly and know it will definitely happen.

In the next chapter, I will explain exactly how you can achieve this for them.

Five

Acquiring Property

In Chapter 2, I told you how to look on the property portals to spot motivated sellers. As a summary reminder, it's about the property pictures (or lack of them), the description, and the estate agent being used to promote the sale.

Many estate agents and solicitor firms will not understand what I am about to explain to you and their negative response could put doubt in your mind. I have successfully used these strategies with selected agents and lawyers and it has worked perfectly.

LESSON TEN: Be careful who you listen to and who you take your advice from

You will have heard the phrase, "You don't know what you don't know," and this is, I believe, the reason why you may be challenged. This is a specialist area of property acquisition and is outside of the norm that society is used to doing.

Let me explain what I mean with an example that is unrelated to property. A typical person studying medicine will have received strong grades at A-Level, gone to a good university, and has taken about six years to become qualified as a Doctor. They start off as a junior doctor and continue to study to move up the ranks.

Therefore, a GP (general practitioner) is a doctor who has many years of training already completed and they are medically very competent. However, for all of their knowledge, they will still refer you to a doctor who has a specialism in a particular area of medicine, for example, heart, eyes, bones/joints, etc.

This is true in specialist property investing, too. I have a list of what I call experts who are part of my Power Team as they understand these strategies (you will find a QR code for my "Power Team" at the back of this book).

If a solicitor were to say to you "That seems awfully risky to me", it could easily unnerve you and stop you in your tracks. Be careful who you take your advice from and make sure they have the background to advise you with this specialism.

By the way, a solicitor is not there to tell you whether you can or you can't. They are not qualified to give you any financial advice. Their role is to assist you with what you decide that you want to do, in a legal manner.

However, the solicitor does have a duty of care to their client, and if in their legal opinion, they believe a transaction is not in their client's best interest, they will make this clear to them.

So here we go... I believe this is the exciting bit of the content and the part where you hear the workable ways to acquire your property.

As mentioned earlier, access to information on one of our Discovery Days is at the back of this book to further what I'm about to explain, if you feel that it is needed.

Purchase Lease Option

A Purchase Lease Option (PLO) is a legal contract made up of three documents.

The first is the Option Agreement which gives you the right to buy a property from the owner for an agreed price on or before a stated date in the future. As well as this right to buy, the agreement also says you are not obligated to purchase it if you change your mind.

This means that if the owner agrees to do a PLO, you can 'try before you buy' with regards to the property and if it's not suitable, you are allowed to hand it back to them. Now, even though you CAN walk away, I personally never go into a contract like this without having the intention to go through with purchasing the property. I think this is the ethical thing to do.

The second document is a Management Agreement and it states who (between you and the owner) is responsible for doing things in regard to the property. This includes insurance, maintenance, bills, how the property will be used, refurbishment, etc.

This is agreed between the two of you and can be different for every seller, as it's based on their (and your) circumstances and needs.

The third document is a Power of Attorney (POA) and this grants you (being the Option Agreement owner) the required authority to sign any documents (with the exception of a mortgage), after the contract is active, on behalf of the owner.

The reason for this POA is that once the problem for a motivated seller has been solved for them, and they've started their new life somewhere, it could become difficult for you to go through with buying the property if they are not cooperative or available. This is prevented by them willingly giving you the right to sign on their behalf.

To be clear, this POA only relates to the property and is not related to any other aspects of their life or finances. It's also not - and is different from - a Lasting Power of Attorney.

There are financial considerations required in order to enter into a Purchase Lease Option. I will discuss more about the fees involved later in this chapter. For now, I just want to explain an overview of paying for a PLO.

The actual Option Agreement becomes valid (when signed) after paying an agreed fee. This will be a minimum of £1 (one GBP) and can be any amount above this, as agreed in your negotiation with the owner.

The Management Agreement will detail how much is paid by you to the owner in order to rent (lease) their property from them.

There is no fee usually paid for using a Power of Attorney except for any legal costs needed.

You will also need to pay your specialist solicitor to prepare the PLO. The owner will also need their own specialist lawyer to represent them. This is very important - both sides (you and them) should take independent legal advice about entering into an agreement together. This should then clarify that both parties fully understand what they are entering into including the arrangements being granted to each other.

There are many benefits to both you and the property owner for agreeing to enter into a Purchase Lease Option.

From the seller's point of view, remember they are motivated for some reason to get rid of their house and are willing to do so. Maybe they've run out of ideas and have already explored the usual routes to dispose of their housing liability.

For you, there is the ability to acquire the property and make it your new home. You do not need to get a mortgage yet and this also means you don't need to find the hefty deposit funds that many mortgage lenders require.

In my experience - and yours too, probably - paying the mortgage amount each month would be less than what people are paying in rent. It's just finding the large deposit that is the prohibiting factor. This huge money down payment is often not needed when entering into a PLO.

If the current owner has a mortgage on the property (they often do have a loan secured against it, but not always) you, as part of the agreement, take over paying the mortgage on their behalf. You could say you "babysit" their mortgage for them.

Remember - they want to get away from their property and become free from paying the mortgage (if any), so having someone else taking responsibility for this is attractive to them.

Depending on who their mortgage provider is, you may need to have Consent To Let (CTL) agreed with their lender. They, the property owner, will need to arrange this albeit you can assist them in the process as they will not know what to do. Obviously, though, the mortgage is private to them and the lender will not discuss any detail of this financing with any unauthorised third parties.

This Consent To Let then gives the owner permission to rent out the property to you. It sort of transfers a residential mortgage into a Buy to Let (BTL) mortgage. Should the owner have an existing BTL loan on the property (for example, if the house you are taking over is an existing rental property owned by a landlord), by nature of already being a BTL product, their mortgage should not need Consent To Let.

Residential mortgage lenders, in my experience, are open to granting CTL if they know the reasons behind the request. I know three ways that lenders have previously granted their permission:

1. "Yes, under the described circumstances, go ahead".

2. "Yes, go ahead after paying us an admin fee of... (whatever they stipulate)".

3. "Yes, but we will increase the annual mortgage percentage to... (whatever they request)".

To be clear, a mortgage lender does not need to grant permission - it is at their discretion. If you don't have their authority, and still go ahead with entering into a PLO, there may be a breach of the mortgage lender's terms and conditions.

I suggest you should also make your Option Agreement assignable, and you need to specifically agree on this with the owner and ask your solicitor to include this clause in the document.

Making a PLO assignable means that you, as the Option holder, have the right (if you so wish) to pass the ownership of the agreement onto someone else. The new Option owner could even pay you a fee for acquiring the rights to the property.

The Management Agreement (MA) details what can and cannot happen to the property while you manage it on behalf of the owner.

You will probably want to upgrade the interior and/or the exterior of the house. You might even want to reconfigure the rooms, extend into the garden or loft, or landscape the outside space.

These changes are possible, so long as the PLO allows whatever you do, and they are included in the document. The reasons you would want to make any changes are to suit your personal décor preferences, and also to enhance the property value.

The MA also says who is responsible for repairs. I generally take on the full responsibility because I plan on the property becoming mine in the not-too-distant future, and this is a huge benefit to the owner who (remember) wants to be rid of the house.

It's important to insure the property building(s) and land, and because you are not yet the owner, you will probably not be able to do this on your own. I get around this by making sure the MA states that the owner will insure the property in both his/her name along with my name and that any monies coming from an insurance claim are granted to me, to be used to fix the insured problem.

The length of the Option Agreement is determined between you and the owner. There is a little bit more work required by your solicitor should the term be seven years or more and they should know to take care of this for you.

You do need to think carefully about the length of your agreed Option period. If the owner has an interest-only mortgage, this amount needs to be repaid before a certain time. So your Option cannot be beyond this date because the mortgage lender will want the loan paid back to them.

I base my Option term on what I intend to do with the property (with regards to upgrading and adding value to it), balanced with whether I think the property market price will go up or down, and with my own circumstances for when I plan to be in a position to get my personal mortgage.

However - and this is very important - you do need to be mindful of the time passing by and the end of the Option period approaching. If you go past this time, the control of the property (as stipulated in the agreement) is transferred back to the owner, and any monies invested or changes made to the property belong to them. There is no recompense to you.

This has happened to others, and now that I've made you aware of it, I'm sure it will be on your radar, and all important dates are diarised by you, so you don't miss out on the benefit of your Option.

At the relevant time during the Option period, the owner sells their property to the purchaser by 'exercising' the Option. This means the agreed method shown in the document is followed to either buy the house as originally intended, or sell the house to someone else.

I've deliberately referred above to selling the house to someone else, as this is another benefit of an Option Agreement. Your intention at the start is to acquire the property to eventually buy it and have your first officially owned property.

If your circumstances change over time though, the agreement allows you to find someone else to buy the property. You have permission, written in the document, to agree to a sale with another person. The house owner is required to give you all reasonable assistance in making this happen.

If the original owner is selling the house to the new buyer, and your Option Agreement states this, you can receive any difference in monies made within the sale proceeds. For example, if you have agreed that your right to acquire the house from the owner is set at £200,000, and later you find a buyer at £275,000, you will gain the difference of £75,000 less any fees payable.

Should you sell the property in this way, the amount of money you receive (the difference between the selling and buying price) is counted as taxable income and you should take advice from a suitable Tax Advisor about how this affects your circumstances.

Even though I've explained one way of how you can make money from a property using a PLO (and there are many other ways), the whole aim of this book is to help first-time buyers to get onto the property ladder, with no more wasted rent. So let's continue on this journey.

A Purchase Lease Option starts off as a blank sheet of paper. We call this the Heads of Terms (HoTs) and this is the form you and the property owner use to capture the exact terms you both agree upon, along with the property address, your details, their details, the Option term, Option fee, and any special arrangements such as who is paying for what, etc.

When the HoTs are fully completed, this is then given to your solicitor to prepare your PLO (there is a sample copy of a Heads of Terms form at the back of this book).

Remember that a PLO "gives you the right to buy a property from the owner for an agreed price on or before a stated date in the future".

I've already discussed "noting the stated date in the future". Let's look at ideas for how to find the "agreed price".

There are many different ways of deciding this price. In fact, far more than I could ever think of putting in this book. I'm going to explain a few of the ways I have used, as I think one of these methods will be useful to help you in securing your first property.

When you are buying anything in life, it's quite natural to want to pay as little as possible. There is nothing wrong with this thinking, although I would like to expand that thinking to look at a PLO in another way.

You see, as I described in Chapter 1, property prices are cyclical but with a shortage of houses to live in, over time there is an upward trend. This means that today's market price is more than likely to be a discounted price in the future.

It's worth reading that last sentence again to understand its meaning fully.

If you offer 100% of the house value, it represents a great deal for the seller because they are agreeing to receive the price in today's market, just like they would if they had sold their house. However, remember this house, for whatever reason, is not selling and they need to let it go and walk away.

Over time, let's assume you've agreed to a five-year Option period, and let's say you've upgraded the kitchen and bathroom or simply redecorated and changed the carpets. Your actions have increased the value of the property, and it's now worth more than you agreed in your Option paperwork. This becomes your gain (or equity).

Here are some examples of PLOs I have done. I will deliberately keep them vague to protect the identity of any owner because their circumstances are personal to them.

PLO Example One:

A person was facing repossession and they contacted me. It turned out that it was their former family home, and for very sad personal reasons, they decided they couldn't live there anymore but were not ready to sell the house. So, instead, they rented it out.

The tenants eventually moved out and the owner then realised there was about £10,000 worth of damage done to the property. This work needed to be done before any other tenant would be willing to move into the property.

The problem was that the person didn't have the £10,000 to spend on repairs, and because there was now no rent coming in, the owner couldn't afford to pay their mortgage, so the lender was threatening to repossess it from the owner.

I was able to step in and mediate with the lender for me to take over control of the property using a PLO. I cleared the outstanding arrears, fixed the damage, and rented it out again.

The owner was more than happy to enter into the PLO as it meant they were not repossessed (so they sort of kept their credit score intact). As the damage caused by the previous tenant devalued the property to less than the outstanding mortgage balance, even if they had sold, there was no money left in it for them anyway.

Over a few years, the property price rose and I was able to use the equity I generated to buy the house for the now below-market value purchase price.

PLO Example Two:

I was contacted by a couple who told me that one of them had just been diagnosed with a serious illness. The quality of life for that person would be dramatically increased if they lived by the seaside.

So there was no question about it... they needed rid of their house and didn't really care about its price.

There wasn't a big mortgage left on the property and the lender was very happy to give me Consent To Let when they understood the diagnosis predicament the owners were facing.

I always intend to do things ethically, and so agreed to a PLO where the future purchase was slightly more than the minimum amount they were happy to accept. Yes, I could have bought it cheaper, but I was already (in my view) buying at a fair discounted price in that marketplace and I didn't want to take advantage of their situation.

A light refurb was needed on the property and I then rented it out to tenants to make it their home. Eventually, as prices of property in that area increased, I was able to benefit from the increased equity to refinance onto a mortgage and I now own this place (as part of my portfolio).

PLO Example Three:

A young couple couldn't sell their property as their outstanding mortgage and further secured loans on the house meant they owed more than the value. They were separating and needed to move out to get on with the rest of their lives.

I negotiated a PLO with them and took control of the property. After upgrading the house a little, it was rented out and the rent more than covers the mortgage I'm paying on behalf of the original owners.

In the examples above, on one I could agree to a discount on the market price. On another, I needed to offer the then market value, whilst on the third I had to agree to give more than the property value as the outstanding loans added up to more than the mortgage amount.

In all cases, a Purchase Lease Option worked for both me and the respective owners. They were all motivated sellers, albeit for very different reasons.

The marketing methods I used to source these initial property leads (which I turned into deals) will be discussed more in Chapter 5.

Buying your PLO using a mortgage

Many mortgage lenders, such as your regular high street banks, do not like offering a mortgage on a property you buy for less than its current market value. So, if your PLO property has gone up in value over the years you have controlled it, you need to choose the right mortgage broker to help you (as discussed in Chapter 3).

Let me use a fictitious example to show the principle of how you might refinance a PLO and overcome this problem. If you are financing as a business, you may need a deposit of 25% and a mortgage based on 75% of the market price. As a private individual with the property in your own name, you can often get a mortgage with a 5-10% deposit and a 90-95% mortgage balance (the deposit required will vary from time to time).

We will use a property with a PLO agreed purchase price of £100,000 and a current market value of £140,000 (because the market value has risen over the years).

Instead of a high street bank, you could use a Bridging Lender for a 75% loan. The remaining 25% could be made up of some of your own money, or a loan from a family member or close friend to make up your deposit. If you are borrowing any part of your deposit money, it's important that both the mortgage broker being used and the bridging company know the source of the funds, and the fact that it is not solely your own funds being used. If you're not sure, a Bridging Lender is a commercial finance company that assesses property deals in a different way than a high street bank. They may not be regulated in the same way, which is useful if it helps you to buy a property, but you need to give careful consideration to any lack of consumer protection. It's down to your level of risk-taking. If you know what you are doing, it is likely to be a low risk of going wrong.

Let's say the property is valued by the bridging company surveyor at £140,000 which means you would receive a temporary loan from them of £105,000 and you put in the deposit of £35,000 if we are using the percentages mentioned above. The PLO will be exercised by your solicitor, who then releases £100,000 to the original owner (as part of your PLO agreement) with the balance of £40,000 being paid to you. You then use £35,000 of this to repay the private loan to your close friend or family member, and the remaining balance is used to cover any costs.

This means you can purchase the property using the equity realised in the property to fund your deposit.

PLEASE NOTE: This method of refinancing may or may not be available to you. There might be other ways to refinance your PLO at the time when you need this service. Please make sure it's a legally acceptable process that you choose to use.

Vendor Finance

This is a way where the person(s) selling their house agree to finance it for you. In other words, loan you their own money in order for you to buy it.

I know, you may be thinking that never happens, does it? Well, in the right circumstances, it works really well for both you and them. I'll explain why shortly.

However, when you get your head around how to do this, you will think it so good that you will want to force it to happen all the time. Just like a PLO, Vendor Finance (VF) needs the situation to be perfect for it to be used, and ONLY if the seller is totally happy to use this method of funding.

The easiest way to describe VF is by saying the seller agrees to become the mortgage lender for you. I cannot talk specifically about finance but, to help you, I will look at typical ideas that might be possible if everyone involved is happy.

I was told that about 25% of all owned properties do not have a mortgage on them. The property has been fully paid off. They are what is called "unencumbered".

Think about why someone with no mortgage on the property they are selling is getting rid of that house. It could be to buy another, and if they need all of the money from the sale for their next place, then VF is not suitable.

However, what if they're downsizing and there will be money being released, or maybe it's a property that has been left to them in a will, or they could be moving in with a new partner? I'm sure you can think of other potential scenarios, too.

For this example, I'll talk about a house that has been left to the vendor through a will. They are not looking to move into the house, as they already have a home. They don't want the stress and hassle of renting it out to tenants, so they decide to sell. All is fine so far.

Let's, though, think from the seller's perspective. They're not selling because they need the money, they are just getting away from having the responsibility of an empty home, and more than likely, the cash will just sit in their bank.

How much interest a year will the bank be able to pay that person on the money sitting in their account? I don't know about your bank's interest rates being paid on savings at the moment, but my bank offers a very low, virtually non-existent rate, especially when you factor inflation into the equation.

So what if the seller were to lend you the money, rather than putting it in their bank, and they earn an annual income equivalent to the current mortgage rate - paid to them by you each month? This would generate a much higher return on their money, I should think.

It's an attractive proposition to them, as they're making more money, and it works really well for you because maybe you're not yet in a mortgageable position but will be in the future. That interest paid to the owner should be much less than the equivalent rent on such a property.

Finding properties suitable for PLO and VF

Techniques to find properties using online property portals have already been explained, and these work really well. However, it's easier to use PLO and VF if the property you're after is not yet for sale on the open market. This makes it easier for you to negotiate without having any competition from other potential buyers.

Word-of-mouth is one of the best methods, either by asking everyone you know if they know of any empty properties, or if they know about houses becoming empty soon. Another way to do this would be to tell people on your social media feeds that you are looking for a property of this nature. It's important to keep mentioning it too, as you'd be surprised how people don't see your message.

Another great method is to keep your eyes open in your neighbourhood when you're out and about, maybe walking, jogging, or cycling. You will see places that look empty more easily than driving passed in a car.

If you do find somewhere interesting, you can write a letter or knock on the door and, if you get no response, you can ask the local neighbours. This can be a little nerve-wracking at first, but you soon get used to it, and can even get to enjoy speaking with people.

I find that if the house next door to them is looking shabby and the garden is overgrown, they're usually very keen to help someone move in and tidy up their street scene.

Of course, a property that needs some updating will need you to spend money on it. So this works well if this fits in with your budget. Often the refurbishment can be less than the mortgage deposit.

BIG TIP: Make sure you've negotiated and secured the place to be yours (on a contract) before spending your money on doing it up. Otherwise, the owner is likely to ask for more money seeing as the property now looks lovely following your tender loving care to the building!

If you struggle to become brazen enough to find properties yourself, you can also use local estate agents, and here are some questions to ask them to help you find suitable houses.

1. "Do you have any empty properties?"

Properties are usually empty for one of four main reasons... a deceased estate (probate), a repossessed property, an ex-rental place, or the owner has moved away from the area (say, if they get a job elsewhere).

2. "Do you have any houses that are For Sale and To Let?"

These make great potential PLO properties, as you could probably rent the property now and buy it later.

3. "Do you have any empty properties where there is more than one agent selling them?"

This agent might be more tempted to arrange a sale with you on a PLO because they could lose the chance of getting their commission if the other agent sells it first.

4. "Do you have empty properties that have been on the market for a long time?"

The definition of "a long time" will be up to the estate agent, but the longer they have unsold properties, the more chance the owner will look to other agents to sell.

5. "Do you have any sellers who keep calling your office to see if there's any news on finding a buyer?"

This is a sign of the seller being motivated, and it's really awkward for the estate agent to keep speaking with them without any news about a potential buyer. You could be exactly the person they are both looking for!

The best thing to do is to build rapport with the estate agent and find a way for you to speak with the seller. Some agents don't like you going direct as they think you will stop them from earning their commission. Of course, you want to do the opposite and make sure they get their payment for introducing you as the buyer.

The goal is to listen to the reason the seller wants to sell and find a solution that works in both your and their favour, as well as the estate agents.

To get their interest, one of my opening sentences to the seller is: "I can give you the price you need if you can give me the terms I need." Their reply is often: "How does that work?", or "What do you mean?", and I can then carry on the conversation with them showing an open mind.

To negotiate the best price, I love using the following phrase: "What's the lowest you will take and still be happy"? It's worked many times in agreeing on a price that works for us both. You cannot and should not use this sentence too early in the negotiation.

It needs to be used when you know there's the possibility of an ethical "win/win" deal and you are finalising the purchase price.

Six

Finding Deposit Money

One of the great benefits of a Purchase Lease Option and a Vendor Finance is that you don't need hefty deposit money to get started. You will need access to some money though, because there will be legal fees, maybe estate agent costs, and also some redecoration or refurbishment of the house required.

When you put your mind to it, it's amazing where you find little pockets of money in various places. I don't know if your bank is able to help you, but I do know of lending companies that understand the concept of PLOs and look more favourably at requests from people when lending for this purpose. Of course, your credit rating may influence the decision (we covered details on how you can help yourself with this in Chapter 3).

I'm well aware that some of the following are not applicable to everyone. The intention here is just a prompt for you to think about what might apply to you. Some of them you might feel are controversial:

   1. Selling items you no longer need or temporarily can do

without

2. Small amounts (maybe even large!) of money in former (not now used and not yet closed) bank and savings accounts

3. Family or friends who may support you with a personal loan

4. Inheritance in advance from your parents or grandparents (or favourite aunts and uncles, or godparents)

5. Dormant pensions which have a useful transfer value

6. The children's money box

7. If you work for yourself, retained cash in your business

8. Personal or business loans

9. The seller

10. Credit cards (be careful here!)

11. Sell property leads

12. Bank of Mum & Dad

...and there are many more possibilities you could use.

Let's just look at some of the above, which may have you currently feeling a little uneasy.

Number one is one of the easiest to handle when you understand that you don't need to get rid of anything forever. It's just a temporary move to help you acquire your home. When you're better off financially, you might want to replace what you once had.

Numbers three and four could make you feel like you are begging for money. I say this because that's how I felt at first when I heard about this method. My mindset is now much different. It's important to note that these people are not strangers to you, and presumably, you trust one another.

If there's the possibility of an inheritance coming your way sometime in the future, I think it's a shame to wait for the money because something (which you probably think is very sad) has to happen in order for you to receive what has been left to you in a will. If it's promised to you anyway, it might be good to have a conversation with that person - and I appreciate it's very delicate - about them seeing you put the funds to good use during their lifetime, rather than just sitting in their bank account.

Separate from any inheritance money, many people have little bits of savings put away for a "rainy day," and the interest they are being paid on this money is very low. You could perhaps borrow the money from them, using an agreement between you to document this and be able to pay them a slightly higher interest rate than they're currently getting. This incentivises them and also assists you.

It should go without saying - but I am going to say it anyway - you do need to have a mechanism or plan in place to return these borrowed funds eventually. This arrangement will be between both parties involved and be different in every case.

Number five is often forgotten about as people change from a job where they had a pension in place, and it's now since been frozen. These can have a reasonable transfer value, and you might be able to have access to it if you move it (or them) to a different type of pension. I've successfully done this with two of my previously dormant pensions, and you may want to do this too, after taking your own independent legal advice from someone qualified in this area.

Number six will tug on your heartstrings. The suggestion is not to steal their money, it's to use it as part of an investment to gain a better home for them to benefit from. Plus, you can return that money to them in the future - with interest if you like.

Number seven could be a pot of money you hadn't realised is available to you through a loan from your business. Many successful companies have money retained inside of them as the owner needs to pay tax on it if it's removed. It could be possible to make a director's loan to you.

Number eight will influence your credit rating and ability to get a mortgage. Still, if it's a small loan that you successfully pay back before you exercise your PLO to buy the house using a mortgage, the lender will see it's been repaid, and this may even enhance your rating because they can see you are responsible with your borrowing and paying back.

Number nine is of course using Vendor Finance which we've already talked about in previous chapters.

Number ten is really useful to use if you need some property "doing up" funds to get you going. You may also find that your solicitor allows you to pay for your PLO on a credit card (this is not always possible and depends on the amount involved). This is expensive borrowing though, and you should plan to pay this back really quickly, and ideally within the credit card's interest-free period.

Number eleven is a great way for you to generate income which can help to cover your own costs. If you find a house suitable for use with a PLO, and it eventually doesn't suit your needs, you could pass it on to someone similar to you for them to use. This is known as Deal Sourcing. You can charge a fee for doing this, although you will need to be aware that this income is likely to be taxable, and there could be some legal compliance issues that need addressing should you decide to become a Deal Sourcer.

Number twelve is used quite a lot when parents are in a position to help by donating money from their savings to their children, helping them get onto the property ladder. Even small amounts of money can help.

You may be fortunate and learn that your parents have more stashed away than you realised, and they can gift you the full deposit you need to buy your first place. Simply start a conversation and when appropriate, ask them if they would like to help.

If you are given the full deposit, the mortgage lender will ask your parents to sign to say these deposit funds are a gift, not a loan. This will be done through the solicitor.

Think about other hidden or forgotten assets you may have, such as shares or bank and building society accounts that you haven't used for years. These can all add up to become meaningful deposits.

LESSON ELEVEN: *Finding the money to invest in property requires discipline*

For some people, what I'm about to suggest may not be what they want to hear, but please take this in the spirit that is intended, and that intention is purely to make you think. Please take a look at how you can rethink your daily spending.

Are there some things you could temporarily do without and add to your house-buying fund? Can you save on drive-through coffees? Can you make your own lunch rather than buy ready-prepared food? Can you go out less often? Could you cut back on the type of WIFI, TV subscriptions, and mobile phone contracts that you use?

You will be amazed by how these all soon add up and will start to empower you to save more. Of course, you must still have some treats, but their type and cost could be less pricey. Over time, these new habits will provide you with the disposable income you are looking for and offer you the choice as to whether to save more or buy a little special something as a reward.

There's a phrase that goes something like: "If the prize is worth it, the price you pay for getting it is worth it." In the future, looking back, the memories of the difficult times can get watered down, especially if you have achieved so much more of your dreams.

Section 3: NURTURE

Seven

Adding Value

Now you have acquired your first property, there are many ways that you can enhance its value to increase its price. Remember, prices are cyclical, and with prices going up and down over time, certain properties will be worth more than others because they look better.

As a guide, an ideal property to take on is one that looks like the worst house on the best street. Do not be put off by how the property looks initially. You want a place you can improve to enhance its value.

Your house can be identical in layout to the property next door but more attractive in design and appeal. This is what you need to happen to enhance the equity in the property. Plan for the increase in the house value to be more than the cost of any improvements or changes you make.

Let's consider some of the ways (this is not an exhaustive list) that can be useful to have a major impact on a property's valuation:

One: **Street appeal**

How your property looks from the roadside can have a really big impact on its price. A well-maintained garden, parking space, maybe electric gates, style of windows, gutters, roofline, painting, lighting, etc., all draw people into liking or disliking what they see, and they will also compare your place to the neighbours.

Two: **Redecoration**

Changing carpets and flooring, interior painting, and wallpaper are easy low-priced ways to make the inside of a house stand out.

Three: **Layout**

How you dress the rooms is very important. Using all of the available space creatively captures the imagination of a valuer. The positioning of furniture, pictures, ornaments, and photographs all subliminally count. Rooms need to flow too when people pass through and use them.

Four: **Colour schemes**

The use of colour on walls, doors, skirting boards, and ceilings is very impactful. You may have a flair for this already. There are numerous interior designers available though, and many techniques can be researched and found online.

Five: **Refurbishment**

Upgrading the kitchen, bathroom, and any cloakroom is the most well-known way to make an impact. Done thoughtfully, this doesn't need to be very expensive. You may be able to add a conservatory or orangery to create more living space, and you might improve the value by moving walls and repositioning which room is the kitchen and the living areas. Adding an ensuite is a nice addition to a property too.

Six: **Development**

You can also look to extend the house or convert the garage, basement, and/or loft area to create more usable space. Extensions can sometimes be done under permitted development (which means without the need for full planning permission), and your local council website will have more information to guide you. Some homes may be excluded, for example, Listed Buildings and flats.

Seven: **Maintenance**

Keeping on top of any repairs inside and outside of the property can enhance the house value too. Fence panels can be blown down or begin to wobble in high winds, and doorways, hallways, and landings soon become marked when children, pets, and adults scrape along them. Moving the vacuum cleaner or furniture around also damages the walls. When you live in the space, you probably won't see these blemishes, but a "fresh pair of eyes" will easily spot them.

Eight: **Tech-enabled**

Most people nowadays are highly dependent on using their gadgets and your home could have a greater appeal if you have included the ability to embrace technology. This means planning where to position the WIFI router and ensuring you can access a strong signal in all the rooms and corners of the property. Have plenty of electricity wall sockets positioned in useful places to allow electric items to be used, and these should also include wall plates that allow the use of USB cables. Smart devices can also be programmed to control the heating, lighting, alarm system, CCTV, and drawing curtains, amongst many other things.

Eight

Your Property Ladder

At the start of this book, I mentioned the idea of helping first-time buyers that came to me in 1985, just after my first daughter had been born and I had struggled to get onto the property ladder. The writing was on the wall, and I knew I needed to do something to help my child to have the dream of owning her own home in the future.

This book is the culmination of many years of finding a way that could achieve this goal. I know the techniques inside this book work, and they can work for you too if you REALLY need them to.

I've deliberately chosen the word "need" and not "want" because something you want differs greatly from something you need. There are many things I want, but very few things I need. You will stop at nothing if it's something important to you.

For me, owning my own home was in this "need" category, I didn't like paying what I saw as wasted rent and having nothing to show for that money. That's the reason I called this book 'No More

Rent'. Whilst doing my research, a millennial suggested the title "Rent to Riches", which I agree has a good ring to it, and I like the alliteration.

Still, I didn't want to be associated with anything that implies "get rich quick". It's true that investing in property can generate wealth for you - I have been a catalyst for inspiring many people to do this, but it needs to be done in a considered way and over a period of time.

Buying a first home and then adding value to it, which increases its value, means you can then sell and use the increased equity to buy your next (better or bigger) property. This can be done over and over again to suit your family's needs. At some time in the future, you could then sell and downsize to release any equity gained to improve your lifestyle.

At the time of writing this book, you do not have to pay Capital Gains Tax on any of the profit (or equity) you make when buying and selling your primary residence. This is one of the reasons why many have used the route of buying, improving, selling, buying, improving, selling, etc. to become the owner of a lovely property and maybe even your dream home.

In the beginning, property investing was my hobby. I had a day job that I absolutely loved, and I never thought the day would come when I gave it up and retired. It's important to say that retirement has nothing to do with age - it's the point in your life when you decide you have enough income from your investments not to need to go out for work. If you reach this stage and continue working, that's fine, but there's a difference between wanting to work and having to work.

I recognised the importance of putting money into a pension. Many of us know this is the right thing to do but it's easier said than done; there are always many demands on your income every month. I used to say "There's plenty of month left over at the end of the money", and this might be the same for you.

I was spending a lot of my spare time on the property portals looking at houses and it dawned on me that if I could scrape together the funds to buy a small place, refurbish it, and find a great tenant to rent it from me, this income would cover the mortgage and overheads, such as insurance and the letting agent fee, leaving me excess money each month. If I could then do this again, I would be building a portfolio.

The important thing (when the penny had dropped) was that once I had acquired the property, the excess profit came in twelve times a year (so long as it was rented out). This was far different from my job, where I only got paid if I turned up for work. Property investing meant I worked once (to acquire the place, set it up, and rent it) to be then paid forever. This got me hooked on the concept of property investing!

Another helpful thing is to ensure your mortgage broker owns their own house and invests in property. There is a specialism that brokers like this possess, and you will find their different way of thinking very useful.

Nine

Property Buying Bonus

I hope by now you realise how it's possible for you to acquire your first home. Henry Ford said something along the lines of "If you think you can do a thing or think you can't do a thing, you're right."

You must take the time to plan out how you want your future life to look. If you don't you will be fitting in with the plans of others, and this only works if they match your dreams.

It's well worth striving to buy your own place as the amount you pay for a mortgage is nearly always much less than you will pay to rent the same property.

Everyone generally falls into two categories. Neither is right nor wrong - you just have to be really honest with yourself to know which best describes your mindset. The first category is a "glass half full" type of person, and this will help you enormously. If you fall into the "glass half empty" category, that's okay too, but you may need to push yourself further outside of your comfort zone.

When buying your own property using a mortgage, you also receive the most incredible bonus – and I have probably left it until this final chapter to share that bonus with you.

Whenever a person has funds to invest, a bank or institution will only pay them interest on the amount that they have invested, at their going rate. However, a mortgage lender is different.

The purchase price of a property is made up of a deposit and a loan from the mortgage company. For a first-time buyer, this deposit might be 10% (although it can vary), which means the balance from the lender is 90%. Over time property prices increase if the property is held for a long enough time.

When the market price of this house has gone up in value, the owner (that is YOU) benefits from 100% of this increase in value and NOT just 10% of it, equivalent to the deposit you invested. Yes, the lender is receiving interest paid on the 90%, but the increase in value, in my experience, is far outweighed by that interest amount.

Other house-buying strategies include Shared Ownership. This is where you own 25% of the property for example, and the lender owns the balance of 75% (these percentages can vary depending on how much monthly payment the buyer can afford). In this scenario, you pay the mortgage monthly on the percentage amount you own and you pay additional interest on the balance owned by the housebuilder or lender.

In a Shared Ownership scheme, you can buy more of the share you don't own over time, which is useful to have a low starting point mortgage, BUT if the house price increases, so does the amount you have to pay. For example, if you bought a house for £100,000 which then increased to a value of £150,000 over time, paying 75% of the £150,000 is a lot more money to find than 75% of the original price of £100,000.

This is not an ideal position to find yourself in, although an ownership scheme like this is better than renting as you will at least have some gain if property prices rise.

The government of the day will create its own ways to promote home ownership, and these should be explored as they could suit your circumstances. Please only take advice from those who have *your* interests at heart, and not their own.

Your Next Steps

It's now time to take action.

I hope you realise the difference between being *interested* in having your own property and being *committed* to making it a reality. At the beginning of this book, I asked you to be really honest with yourself and think differently from many other people in order to get the most out of what I have shared with you. With this in mind, I also hope that in your heart of hearts, you have decided which of the above options best describes you now.

If you are excited and want to buy your own home, you will now have enough knowledge to do so. That said, I appreciate why you might be thinking, "What? Can I really do it?". If this is how you are feeling, please read this book again and highlight the important parts that are relevant to where you are right now.

I've used property investing strategies like those explained in this book, and I know they can work. I also remember them feeling very alien to my previous thinking, and in some ways, I held myself back from trying to implement them. PLEASE do not be like this. If I can do it, then so can you.

In fact, I have trained thousands of students to have the courage and confidence to go out there and start buying their own property, and I have been recognised with several awards for doing so.

And now I would like to help you, too, if you will let me. There's more about how this could work below.

Be very careful who you take your advice and counsel from. Is that person authorised to comment... and are they (in their life) where you want to be? My parents were extremely protective of me when I told them about investing in property, and they did try to put me off. When I succeeded, they proudly told everyone how well I had done.

Other family members, and (in my experience) some of your friends and work colleagues will try to dissuade you. You see, other people don't mind you doing well, just so long as you are not doing better than them in most cases.

Don't allow others to hold you back. Instead, lead the way, and they will no doubt follow after a while. Change within a person often comes when they are either seriously inspired or their circumstances have unfortunately deemed them desperate. You can be that inspiration through all the knowledge and experience that you have acquired, and when they want to know more, just tell them to buy their own copy of this book!

You will come across people who say you don't need to buy any courses to help you because there are so many free resources available on the internet. If this is true, I have a question for you to ponder… why are these so-called experts not already millionaires themselves? How many properties does the person giving you their opinion have? Are they truly financially successful?

Yes, there is much information to be found online. Some of it is brilliant and helpful whilst other details are misleading, confusing, and/or only partly true. When it's all new to you, the difficulty is knowing the difference.

Remember, free information is not valued like something you have paid for and invested in.

Your BIGGEST driver and motivation will come from being very clear on your reason why. You must know exactly what it means to have your own home, which you are buying. Sometimes the road to achieving this can become a little bumpy, and it's your determination that will see you through it all.

If you are serious about changing your situation, allowing someone you relate with to guide you is important. Maybe this person is me, along with my team. Discovery Days are held from time to time, and you can find out more on this website: **www.NoMore Rent.uk**

A Discovery Day is where the words written in this book are talked through, brought to life, and your questions are answered. The intention is to empower you to believe you can buy your own property and gain the courage to make this happen.

You might recall my own "reason why" that I explained at the beginning of this book. Not only was I able to help my Daughter buy her own home, but I realised how fulfilling it would be for me to help other first-time buyers to do the same. With this in mind, further mentoring – either on a one-to-one basis or in a group setting - can also be available. You will know after attending a Discovery Day if this option is right for you.

From the bottom of my heart – thank you for reading this book. I hope you have found it fascinating, and I would be delighted if it were to become the catalyst to ignite the necessary desire inside of you.

Have fun finding your own new home using your freshly learned property knowledge, and please take full advantage of the QR codes that appear over the next couple of pages for access to my "Power Team", and also for more information on our "Discovery Days" if you would love to dive into the world of property even further.

If you are a fan of this book, I would be eternally grateful if you could encourage others by giving it a favourable review on Amazon using the QR code on page 97.

My Power Team

You might recall that I referred to my "Power Team" several times throughout this book. I am sharing the details of that team with you to assist with your new-found property knowledge. Please access the list using the QR code below – you will also find the Heads of Terms example document there too.

Discovery Days

I strongly believe that you can acquire your own home by adopting and implementing all of the knowledge within this book. I also recognise that everyone has different learning styles, and this might mean a book alone may not provide the full support that you need, and being within an environment of like-minded people could really help you to accelerate your growth.

At this point in the book, you might have realised that teaching people all about property is a real passion of mine. With all of this in mind, my team and I hold regular "Discovery Days" where we can do exactly that, in that room full of like-minded people that I mentioned above.

If this sounds like something you might need, please don't hesitate to reach out to us. There is no obligation, and you can find out more using the QR code on the opposite page.

[QR code]

Find out more about our Discovery Days here

[QR code]

Kindly leave a book review here

Acknowledgements

Thank you for reading this far through my book. I would like to highlight just some of the people who have helped me with this journey.

My Dad, John Haynes, worked in insurance for most of his working life, and being surrounded by people making claims on their policies made him all too aware of what can and does go wrong in people's lives. This naturally made him a very cautious person. My Mum, Yvonne, always supported the underdog, and her encouragement to anybody and everyone to keep going and achieve through any adversity was an unbelievable gift. I know my parents have given me the right amount of balance to make things happen, no matter the circumstances, with a sprinkling of reality and caution thrown in for good measure. The banter and friendly rivalry with my brothers, Stephen and Patrick, and sister, Julie, also helped to shape me.

Karen, my wife, has been with me for most of my property investing journey and graduated with me from the many training programs we invested our money, time, and effort into to grow our portfolio. Her personality style is the opposite of mine, and it provides us with a balancing dynamic and perspective in our business. Karen runs our property portfolio business, enabling me to free up my time to be with and train others during their property investing journey. Our children, Laura, Henry, and Victoria, have also influenced and balanced our lives with a mix of work, rest, and play.

We can always learn more, and I firmly believe in investing in yourself and continually growing your knowledge. This is why I still, to this day, attend further training and have a coach and mentor to support me with my thinking, fitness, business, and direction. Martin Norbury has been my business guide in preparing and launching this book, and Simon Zutshi has, without a doubt, been the biggest influence on my property investing success. Simon believed in me and allowed me to grow in my knowledge to become the lead trainer in his organisation. This has enabled me to inspire and become the catalyst for thousands of other property investors.

There has also been much admin support during the writing of this book. Bex and Lauren have given a lot of virtual help. I'm also really grateful for my personal assistant, Amy Fitzgerald, who has managed the back office of my book publishing business for me. Amy's attitude, work, energy, support, outcomes, magnanimity, and ethics have been truly AWESOME.

Andy Haynes

LESS EXCUSES,
MORE RESULTS

Printed in Great Britain
by Amazon